The Parent and Carer in School

THE ATTACHMENT AWARE SCHOOL SERIES
Bridging the gap for troubled pupils

Book 1   The Key Adult in School
Book 2   The Senior Manager in School
Book 3   The Key Teacher in School
Book 4   Team Pupil in School
Book 5   The Parent and Carer in School

Other books in the
Attachment Aware Schools Collection®

ATTACHMENT AWARE SCHOOLS COLLECTION®

Attachment in the Classroom
Better Play
Conversations That Matter
Inside I'm Hurting
Little-Mouse Finds a Safe Place
School as a Secure Base
Settling to Learn
Teaching the Unteachable
Teenagers and Attachment
Temper Temper!
What About Me?
What Can I Do With The Kid Who…?
You think I'm Evil

ATTACHMENT AWARE SCHOOL SERIES

Bridging the gap for troubled pupils

Book 5

The Parent and Carer in School

Louise Michelle Bombèr

First published 2016 by Worth Publishing Ltd
worthpublishing.com

© Worth Publishing Ltd 2016

All rights reserved. No part of this publication may be reproduced, stored in a retrieval system or transmitted in any form, or by any means, electronic, mechanical, photocopying, recording or otherwise, without the prior permission of the publishers, nor be otherwise circulated without the publisher's consent in any form of binding or cover other than that in which it is published and without a similar condition being imposed on the subsequent purchaser.

Printed and bound in Great Britain by TJ International,
Padstow, Cornwall

British Library Cataloguing in Publication Data
A catalogue record for this book is available from the British Library
ISBN   9781903269329

Cover and text design by Anna Murphy

For Jane Airey,
who played a significant role
in my journey

Biography

Louise Michelle Bombèr is a specialist Attachment Lead Teacher and a therapist. She has worked for many years with children and young people who have experienced significant relational traumas and losses. Working in many different contexts she is passionate about ensuring these pupils have opportunity to adapt and recover so that they can make the most of all that school offers. She continues to work as a practitioner using Theraplay®, PACE, DDP and sensory interventions to support children and their parents.

Louise is the author of *Inside I'm Hurting*, *What About Me?*, co-author with Dr Dan Hughes of *Settling to Learn* and contributor to *Teenagers and Attachment*. Her work has been greatly influenced by John Bowlby, Dan Hughes, Daniel Siegel, Bruce Perry and Gabor Maté. Louise advises, trains and supports education professionals and families, and is involved in direct work with children and young people in class, in the therapy room and at an allotment project, PLOT 22. She heads up a network which enables Attachment Leads to be trained to provide advocacy and support in individual schools across the UK (attachmentleadnetwork.net).

Acknowledgements

Thanks to Dr Kim Golding for her continued partnership with me, and my long standing supervisor Penny Auton, who has walked alongside me in my professional journey over many, many years. I would like to thank Jenny Peters in the UK and Glen Cooper in the USA for generously providing me with commentary on Circle of Security®, which is such an invaluable resource to all those wanting to make a difference in children's lives.

I would like to honour all those parents and carers that have shared their stories so vulnerably with me over the years as to what it is like to parent these children. I admire you and so wish that your children could see what I see, how much you deeply love them and root for them and how you desire for them to know how much they are valued, special and that they 'belong' to your family. This is so hard for them to take in.

My current TouchBase™ team - Jennie Fellows, Julia Wilde, Keeley de Freese, Becs Uvieghara, Natalie Miller, Tania Druce,

Alice Malorie and Henrietta Kuhudzai for your dedication and commitment to these children; it doesn't go unnoticed. My national trainers, Anne Henderson, Clare Langhorne, Alison Lumley and Helen Wallace who so passionately deliver materials they believe in, whilst continuing as practitioners actively involved with many pupils. All the support assistants and mentors with whom I have journeyed since 2000; together we have learned what is needed.

My editor and friend Andrea Perry who encourages and mobilises me into further creativity. My husband Jonathan Fordham, who often releases me from household responsibilities because he believes in this cause as much as I do. Thanks for holding the fort when I bury my head in books and my laptop! Lucinda and Steve Smith who lead with both gentleness and strength, continuing to be really behind my vision to see dignity restored. Nothing goes unnoticed.

All the brave families who have endured more than many will ever know and yet remain standing clothed in dignity and strength and armed with fierce compassion for their hurting children. May this series of books play some part in raising much needed awareness so that you can take a step back, trusting the schools your children attend to nurture them into all they should have been first time around.

Foreword

I am so pleased to see this guide for parents and carers as part of the **Attachment Aware School Series**. As Louise so clearly explains, Team Pupil would not be complete without the inclusion of parents. Parents through birth, adoption, fostering, residential or kinship care will find this an important map on their journey with their child, helping them to work closely with the school team to make sure that she or he gets the best support possible.

Parents need to find a balance between encouraging their children to take opportunities, and supporting them with the challenges that school can bring. Finding this balance point can be especially difficult when the child has experienced developmental trauma. Learning, trusting adults, peer relationships, aspects of the curriculum which touch on the trauma of the past, managing separation and transition; there are so many potential hurdles that the child has to navigate in the world of school in order to benefit from opportunity. It is hard to imagine how this balance can be reached unless parents and school staff are working closely together, with respect and appreciation between everyone in the team.

When parenting or educating children who have experienced developmental traumas, it is all too easy to become organised by that trauma (as the dominant factor in the situation), and this can get in the way of healthy working together. At these times, all of us including parents and educational staff can lose our ability to reflect. Trauma shuts down our thinking, meaning we respond to the child and to each other without understanding. Louise is helping us to be 'trauma informed'. With this understanding, parent and educator can consciously work together to help the child to discover his own mind, to organise his experience, and eventually to put into words what he is experiencing. This increases the capacity for regulation and reflection, allowing the child to be in a receptive state for learning. The starting point for this positive process is close working together, leading to a shared understanding of each other and of the child.

Clear, practical and grounded in compassion for the parent, this guide will be invaluable in helping parents to take their place within the team to travel this journey together, and in helping the school staff to understand and facilitate parents to do so.

Within the **Attachment Aware School Series** as a whole, Louise is providing a guide which will help all members of Team Pupil build relationships and connections with each other. Ultimately, this can provide the children with the connection and safety that they need. Parents and educators working together can truly provide healing environments which ultimately will help children benefit from opportunities, overcome challenges and to become all that they are capable of.

Kim S. Golding, 2016

The Parent and Carer in School

Please note: In this book I reference material from my earlier publications, using acronyms for their titles for accessibility. These books form a key resource for developing attachment awareness and trauma informed interventions in schools, and provide background reading for the **Attachment Aware School Series.**

Inside I'm Hurting	(2009)	(**IIH**)
What About Me?	(2011)	(**WAM**)
Settling to Learn (with Dan Hughes)	(2013)	(**STL**)
Key Adult in School	(2015)	(**KAiS**)
Key Teacher in School	(2016)	(**KT**)
Senior Manager in School	(2016)	(**SM**)
Teenagers & Attachment (*in* Perry, Ed.)	(2009)	(**TA**)

Contents

Introduction 1

PART 1 Strengthening parents and carers' attachment awareness 13

Strengths of children with attachment aware parents and carers 15

Good questions from attachment aware parents and carers 16

A Pyramid of attachment aware and trauma informed support 21

PART 2 The parent and carer and Team Pupil 25

Responsibilities of parents and carers 27

10 things others in Team Pupil say about parents and carers 28

continues/...

PART 3	**Facilitating the best outcomes**	**33**
	A Roles and responsibilities	34
	EXERCISES to build self-awareness	60
	B Working as a team with school staff	64
	10 comments from other parents and carers	68
	C Stressors and calmers	71
	D Mapping progress	74
	E Transition planning and preparation	75
	10 comments from children and young people	79

Glossary	81
References	91
Useful contacts	97

Introduction

In the past, schools used to pay lip service to **parents and carers** through formalised meetings such as parent evenings, annual reviews, PEPS … those days are gone. We now realise how important it is to work in close partnership with you, to co-work. To recognise you as an integral part of your child's learning process.

I know that you are the expert on your child. You have seen him at his best and worst. You know what makes him tick, and what stresses him out. You know what he lets the world see, and what he keeps hidden, or you may have some idea. You hold the story of what he has lived through so far.

And I also know that at school, we sometimes see some other parts of the fragmented picture of your child. We now realise that if we work together, we can understand more, and see more, and that this is essential if your child is going to be able to settle into our schools, feel safe and secure, and

The Parent and Carer in School

trust us, the staff, to help him or her learn. We realise that there is a direct correlation between emotional growth and wellbeing, and learning.

So it makes absolute sense that you the **parent or carer**, and we the school staff, get to know each other - well. Please come and share your story, so that we have some clues as we start working with your child. Then, as we go forward, please come alongside us and share how your family life is going. And we will share with you what we're doing in school, what we think will help your child make the most of what is on offer here. We are not here to judge. We are here to attempt to put the pieces together, so we can ensure we take your whole child into account and support his or her recovery from the trauma and loss he or she has experienced. We realise our responsibility now: we recognise the UN agreement on the rights of the child*: and we want to work with you to do our best for your child's present and future.

The pocket-sized book you are reading now is part of the **Attachment Aware Schools Series**. The series has come about in response to an increasing understanding amongst school staff that security, through the experience of secure

---

*States Parties shall take all appropriate measures to promote physical and psychological recovery and social reintegration of a child victim of: any form of neglect, exploitation, or abuse ... Such recovery and reintegration shall take place in an environment which fosters the health, self respect and dignity of the child.
  (Article 39 of UN declaration of the Rights of The Child 1959)

relationships, is necessary for every child to be able to settle to learn and make the most of the educational opportunities out there. It's only when your child's **attachment system** - their need for safe and stable relationship - is attended to, that their **exploratory system** - their ability to be open to learning - can really into come into play.

Some children may have learned security outside school through their experience of relationships to date - others, sadly, may not. Some pupils find settling into learning incredibly difficult, especially those who have a history of not being looked after, attended to, responded to sufficiently, or often or well enough; a history of neglect, traumatic experience or significant loss. If circumstances have ruptured or inhibited the development of an internal, 'felt' sense of security, then children often experience huge anxiety - sometimes unnoticed by those of us observing. Knowing your child's history, perhaps you recognise him or her as belonging, to some degree, in this group.

Pupils like this are not in a position to learn or take up the huge range of opportunities available to them in school YET. So, in school, we now recognise that we must first address their need for security and stability - by providing them with a consistent, reliable, empathic attuned relationship in school, to parallel the secure relationships they have with **parents and carers** like you, at home. Only then can we expect these pupils - your children - to make progress with

The Parent and Carer in School

learning, and to fully engage with their school life.

On really difficult days, even the most securely attached child or adult may find learning a struggle. So this series of pocket books endorses the view that if a school is fully attachment aware, all children and staff will benefit, as will the pupils' **parents and carers**. Ideally all staff will have attachment aware training as their foundation, and will find ways to share this with you. If they don't yet, but you have learnt about attachment yourself, please go ahead and share your knowledge and expertise, remembering that most staff are doing the best they can with what they know. Hopefully with your support they'll appreciate that for some pupils, a specific, targeted relational intervention, such as I'm describing in this book and in the Series, *will be a lifeline*.

In the **Attachment Aware School Series**, we advocate having a small tight team around each specific pupil. So we will have Team Lee, Team Grace, Team Aiden ... four or five people in different positions of responsibility in the school, all believing in and rooting for your child.

> Having several good attachment relationships predicts better self-control, behaviour and relationships.
>
> Belsky et al 2007

If your child is in the primary phase, this team will usually be made up of a Key Adult (*see* p.8), a back-up adult if appropriate, the class teacher, and a Senior Manager (SENCO or INCO, the Assistant Head or the Head). If your child is in secondary, this would usually be the Key Adult, the form tutor, a subject teacher (in a subject your child has strengths in or enjoys) and one or two Senior Managers (the Head of Year, the SENCO/INCO and the Assistant Head). In addition to this school-based team, your child needs to know that you, their **parent or carer**, is on board with their education, actively working in tight partnership with their unique team.

With all this in mind, there are five books in the **Attachment Aware Schools Series**, each reflecting the different roles of the individuals in your child's Team (one book for each member of the team), and one for you. The Series is written to help this valuable community work well together and hold the pupil in our minds, shoring him or her up when necessary, serving as an anchor so that anxieties can be relieved; freeing up the possibility of your child becoming all they were intended to be, first time around. Throughout each book you'll find some key words are highlighted in bold, and you'll find all of these in the **Glossary** on p.81.

This particular book is intended for you as a **parent or carer** of a child or young person who has experienced significant **relational traumas** and losses in their early life, and who has been identified as potentially benefiting from a close relationship with the educational staff in Team Pupil, especially with a Key Adult.

The Parent and Carer in School

Parents and carers have such a significant role in working together with Team Pupil. You are the main person (or people) in your child's life, their **primary attachment figure(s)**. How you relate to your child's school and education - to the staff, the school, and all the aspects of the learning involved, will be carefully watched by your child with great interest. They need the message from you that you trust the adults they'll meet in school, and that you trust the safety, security and stability of the learning context that has been chosen for them. Otherwise, they'll pick up any hesitancy you might have, and regrettably, that can fuel the heightened anxiety and alarm they already carry with them, because of their early life experiences. As I'm sure you know, these children often assume the worst. So be aware that your responses will need to be even more measured than usual! You can play a significant part in paving the way for your child to feel safe enough to explore, safe enough to have a go and safe enough to take the risks required in learning. School is a big ask. You are their best ally.

It will be your role to remain calm, grounded and confident in all areas of school life, supporting your child to start to realise that there are many other kinds of grown-ups out there in the world, different to the ones who haven't cared from them properly. You are the secure base from which your child can have the confidence to venture out into new uncharted territories. When they know you are really there for them, your support will enable your child to fly. There are so many new and exciting opportunities and possibilities out there. As **parents and carers**, there is so much you can do to encourage them to take small steps forward.

When your child wants to give up or maybe not even face the crowds, it will be your job to cheer them on from the side lines. Let your child know you believe in them and all they can be. Dream big dreams for them. Remind them how far they have come and all the things they've become stronger at along the way, such as perseverance. In some cases, as I'm sure you know, it's almost a miracle that some children have made it this far. They've survived despite having lived through toxic and overwhelming stress as very young children, with very limited resources, with developmental immaturities and often little or no support. Please let them know that now, they are not alone: and that together you will get through whatever it is that is causing them concern.

As a **parent or carer**, you'll need to stay connected to Team Pupil. I hope you'll soon realise the value of sharing what you've noticed about what stresses your child, and what calms your child (*see* p.71). One of your roles will be to support staff to make connections between the past and the present, for example when your child is stressed by something in school that you know reminds them of something difficult that happened in their early life. The staff might not spot this, might not recognise what is going on; but you might, and your role is to knit things up together with Team Pupil so

The Parent and Carer in School

that your child's behaviour is understood as an expression of his or her distress, not of being 'bad' or disrespectful. Your role will to raise awareness of your child's needs with the staff, carrying the story of what she or he has lived through. Taking time to understand the school ethos and culture, the staff and their approaches will all play a big part in supporting your child to feel safe enough to settle to learn in this context.

In the type of support work described in the **Attachment Aware Schools Series**, the Key Adult is encouraged to become an **additional attachment figure** for your child, like having an extended family member in school: whilst you remain the **primary attachment figure**. The Key Adult has the closest relationship with you as the **parent or carer** of a troubled pupil.

Key Adults are usually members of support staff - teaching assistants (TAs), individual needs assistants (INAs), emotional literacy support assistants (ELSAs) or mentors from the main school staff. Key Adults prepare themselves to be the best they can for those pupils who have experienced toxic stress anytime from pregnancy onwards, and/or have had compromised or disrupted relationships/connections with adults in their early years.

We now know that a history of **relational trauma** and loss needn't be a life sentence of **insecure attachments**, **developmental vulnerability**, low educational outcomes and a compromised future. Children and young people can learn security and can negotiate and consolidate the necessary developmental milestones; but they need us all alongside them to do so. Education from 5 to 16 is compulsory in the UK, and so these children and young people will be in school for many weeks, terms and years. If they have been wounded 'within relationship', it makes sense for us to prioritise relationships as a way of helping them, since relationship is the necessary vehicle for supporting adaptation and recovery.

> For many children and young people, a sense of connectedness with just one adult … is enough to end their deep sense of alones, isolation, not belonging, not being understood. Sunderland 2015, p.19

We now know that both emotional growth and wellbeing are directly linked to learning. We also know that the more a child or young person experiences quality connection with mature adults, the more mature his brain becomes. So the Senior Manager in Team Pupil will ensure that time and resources are invested into providing stable relationships for your child and others who have also experienced trauma and loss, as well as supporting other staff to become attachment aware and trauma informed.

We also know from neuroscience that the richer experiences of relationship these pupils have, the more complex the neural pathways and connections in their brains will be, meaning that relationship brings integration. And integration brings

The Parent and Carer in School

health - physical, mental and emotional health. And richer experiences of relationships and more complex brain systems will mean your child will be able to engage in more complex thinking, relating and being. This is the way ahead for all of us who take our pupils' and our children's wellbeing and development seriously.

> Let's shift from a behavioral view of pupils to a relational one ... focusing on trying to understand what their behaviour means [or communicates].
> Hughes & Bayline 2012, p.8 (my parantheses)

Up until recently, it was thought that the responsibility to support the mental health and wellbeing of these children and young people lay solely with their **parents or carers**, social workers and therapists. However, I know first-hand from many years of experience out in schools how powerful a Key Adult relationship and an assigned Team Pupil can be within the educational context.

Key Adults who are physically and emotionally present, attentive, attuned and responsive, provide the ground for these children and young people to thrive. And those Key Adults who also employ *playfulness*, communicate *acceptance*, engage *curiosity* and show *empathy* (PACE - Hughes 2006, *and see* Book 1, *in this series*, **KAiS**) can actually support these pupils into new learning, development and opportunities. The possibilities are endless!

It can make such a significant impact if a **parent or carer** has a positive, open working relationship with Team Pupil. I know of some Key Adults who have actually become very good friends with the family and still continue to meet up long after children have moved on from their school. We encourage this! All the staff who are working in an attachment aware and trauma informed way know the importance of boundaries and will keep to their professional role in terms of what they talk about and where they might arrange to meet with you.

But sadly I also know of some **parents and carers** who have communicated angst and worry concerning their children in school. Many of their children have opted to stay home: it may be that their parents' anxiety has reinforced the child's existing fears about grown-ups. It is only natural to be concerned that a staff team will 'get' your child, and be able to work with them and their very particular needs. Staff are only human, and so sometimes there will be a issue that needs to be addressed. If you do have concerns, I hope that you will feel able to work with the school, and if you have doubts and anxieties about what's happening, that you'll find Team Pupil accessible, welcoming and supportive, and able to put your mind at rest.

> Teacher-student attunement is not a 'nice addition' to the learning experience but a core requiremernt.
>
> Cozolino 2013, p.18

The Parent and Carer in School

A NOTE ABOUT CONSULTATION

Each of us needs to be clear as to the boundaries of our role and responsibilities. There are occasions when attachment aware interventions in school will not be sufficient, and a trauma informed practitioner may need to be involved for specialist assessment, advice and interventions. Of course you will be very much involved with this process, or can request it. The school will have acess to a network of specialist therapists with complex trauma/**developmental trauma** expertise, who can work with staff to increase their care-giving capacity. Everyone can work together to give your child the permanency they need (*and see* pp.21, 30).

In all this support work, I strongly advocate that everyone involved stays connected to others who are in similar roles. So for example, in Brighton & Hove, we run an Adopters Supporting Education groups (ASE) for parents to journey together. At various points during the school year we discuss helpful pointers and share practical strategies together. We have discovered that so many parents and carers out there are keen to do the right thing, to ensure that they provide the right kind of support during their child's education. Support networks facilitate confidence and pave the way for children to 'tap into their **exploratory systems**' - in other words, feel so safe and secure at home and at school that they can open to all the joy and excitement of learning. This is our joint challenge and opportunity.

Part One

Strengthening attachment awareness

The aim of this book is to support you as a **parent or carer** to realise how valuable you are as a supporter of your child's education, and to discuss specific things you can do in order to help their learning process. I advocate the creation of Team Pupil for every child who has experienced **relational trauma** and loss, and an opportunity to learn trust and security through the relationship with and **relative dependency** on a consistent adult in school who offers sensitive care (the Key Adult). This will enable your child to settle to learn. Here I'll outline the essential role you can play in this.

Many **parents and carers** don't immediately understand why we might need to encourage 'dependency', and discourage what might look like independence; they initially think that we should be encouraging greater maturity. However, my experience is that many children who have

The Parent and Carer in School

experienced profound trauma and loss have had to 'grow up' too soon, and because of their early life experiences, have moved into a false maturity, pseudo-independence.

This type of maturity can look quite cute when a child is five or six, but left unchallenged can be a nightmare to undo at the adolescent phase. If we remind ourselves of what they might have learned when younger, about grown-ups, we realise how important it is that we help these children update what adults *should* do: bring safety, support regulation of big emotional states, sensations and feelings, and help children experience joy.

I'm sure you're doing all you can to overcompensate for this whilst they are with you being parented! And we need to do the same in school. Don't be fazed by their size or age - just remember what they have learned about grown-ups. Gently challenge distorted perceptions that still affect them now. We want your children to trust most grown-ups, to follow the lead of grown-ups in the education system, and to relinquish some control to the grown-ups in school so that they can be fully freed up to be a child and to learn. It's a big ask. You can really help.

I know that parenting or caring for a child who has experienced **relational trauma** and loss in their early lives can be rewarding but also immensely challenging at times. I also realise that at first, the way of working and collaborating with your child's Team that I describe here and throughout the **Attachment Aware Schools Series** may seem very new and possibly alien for you.

But what I also know, from all the families I've worked with during the last 15 years, is that our collective relentless care and patience pays off, over time. It is a case of persevering and not giving up. Easy to say, I know! But please remember that we won't necessarily be able to see some of what is being invested into our children's lives, possibly for quite a while. Just like us, it can take them time to process whatever differs from what they expect or find familiar. We're all learning together. And what I've repeatedly observed amongst the children and teenagers of attachment aware **parents and carers** are the following strengths and feelings:

Strengths of children with attachment aware parents and carers

> Valued ☆ Understood ☆ Robust
> A sense of belonging
> **Heard ☆ Empathic ☆ Calm**
> Connected to
> **Their trust strengthening**
> Secure ☆ Safe ☆ Integrated
> **Known ☆ Advocated for**
> A sense of stability ☆ Takes risks required in learning

The Parent and Carer in School

Good questions from attachment aware parents and carers

↳ *What should I say to my child about why they are receiving support at school?*

Explain that some of us are lucky enough to get our own team of supporters to ensure we are as comfortable as possible in school, and can make the most of all the opportunities there. Explain they will be watching your child's back and their Team is their first port of call if he or she is unhappy or excited about anything.

↳ *Should 'backclassing' ever be considered due to my child's developmental vulnerability?*

Sometimes. In some cases it may be helpful to repeat a year, especially if there will be more opportunity for play. Many children who have **developmental vulnerabilities** don't necessarily 'fit' our school systems and structures. In every case we need to think about the individual. Other possibilities might include nurture provision, shared timetable with early years' input, or an enhanced curriculum. If we are really considering an individual child's needs we should be able to creatively bring the support to them, wherever they are!

↳ *What if my child gets really close to their Key Adult?*

Celebrate! This is a good sign. We want to be encouraging closeness. Maybe think about the Key Adult as a kind auntie or uncle, and the helpful role they might play in your child's development. It is a similar type of relationship. These children need 'good enough' relationships with adults at home and school if they are to recover. They need the opportunity to practice dependency with sensitively attuned grown-ups so they can recognise the difference between healthy and unhealthy relationships with adults before relating to their peers.

However, you are right to be cautious if you have spotted the Key Adult being a bit unboundaried. All Key Adults are strongly advised to hold their boundaries, especially around not talking about their own personal histories and current home contexts inappropriately. We are asking for a personal and professional relationship to be established. If you are at all concerned, do ask to speak to the Senior Manager in Team Pupil, as they are overseeing all the work going on.

↳ *What will the other children think about my child receiving this type of support?*

If questions are asked, it's probably because the school hasn't done enough work yet on including and celebrating difference and diversity. It may also suggest a lack of training; perhaps other pupils are picking up a bit of hesitancy from some of the staff who know less about attachment than Team Pupil. Our classes watch everything and don't miss a trick! Encourage your child's school to be truly inclusive. Recommend whole school communities sign up to inclusion though developing a strong ethos and more importantly, a

The Parent and Carer in School

strong practice through training and reading. Recommend whole school communities realise the full benefits of being inclusive for their own personal and work lives.

↳ *What if other parents complain about my child's behaviour?*

Meet together with Team Pupil as soon as you can if this happens. Don't attempt to deal with it alone! Sadly there's still a lack of knowledge in the wider community about the impact of trauma and loss. Many people don't realise that not all behaviour is because a child is disobedient or naughty: but that many behaviours communicate a deep distress. I know of many a family feeling evaluated and judged in the supermarket, the park, at the station, on the driveway, on holiday … I could go on, and I'm sure you could too! There is a lot of work to do in health promotion across the board on this. We can play our small part by offering training and drop-ins to parents so that they can have access to facts and figures and understand why we all do what we do. To encourage you, remember it was only a while back that folk realised what autism was. It's taken years of work to support the community to really understand. It's the same with the impact of trauma and loss on behaviour. We'll get there.

↳ *Should we be focusing on homework outside of school?*

This is something that you and Team Pupil need to discuss together. There are many pupils out there who need challenge to be reduced and nurture to be increased, which may mean less or no homework and more play! Think about the 'big asks' of school (*see* **WAM**) ,and think whether, right now, there is any way you could encourage your child to experience more of what they haven't had much of because of their early life experiences, for example play, cuddles, fun and so on. At the beginning of the recovery journey, we need to prioritise over-compensatory nurture, and only gradually increase challenge over time.

↳ *Should we ever request a reduced timetable or an alternative curriculum for our child?*

Sometimes this may need to happen. We all know that these pupils have spikey progress profiles. Something might happen on the outside or inside of a child's life that causes some more instability that unsettles them again for a while. At these times, increase nurture and take down the challenge. These periods will only be seasons, but we do need to be prepared to be flexible and creative at different points along the journey. If a reduced timetable or enhanced/alternative curriculum is suggested, ensure that it is full of your child's interests and strengths (their resiliences!)

↳ *Do we need to encourage the school to start withdrawing support in preparation for secondary or college?*

No!! Please strongly recommend that instead of reducing support at times of transition that the school actually

The Parent and Carer in School

considers either keeping the same support or increasing it. Times of transition and change activate our stress systems. The stress systems of these children are already fried! They *particularly* need our support at these times. Why do you think there are so many exclusions in school, and so many behaviour units and PRUs get most of their referrals, at the end of the terms?! Let's stagger endings and beginnings as much as possible (*and see* **WAM, STL, TAA** *and below*, p.75 *for more on transitions*).

↳ Should we consider special school provision over mainstream?

This is a hard call and a decision you will need to make together with Team Pupil. However, to help you in that decision-making process, please consider that many of our special schools are made up of children who have experienced relational trauma and loss, or still are, right now. So many of our pupil referral units and special schools have to manage safeguarding risks, working closely with Social Services. If, as a parent or carer, one of your roles is to be a stress regulator for your child (help them manage stress - *see* p.43) - think about which school is going to be less stressful for him or her, paying particular attention to their 'faulty nervous system' which is so over-easily triggered (*see* **IIH**, *and below* p.72). We do not want your child's anxiety tipping into feeling overwhelmed or terrified. Sadly, other students can activate our children's alarm systems because of their own traumatised state and faulty alarm systems.

The more regulated we can keep our children, the better! Whatever you decide, I'm including my Pyramid of Support for you here (*see below*), so that you can ensure the school you choose for your child engages in appropriate types of training, support and links up with relevant outside agencies to provide the best possible care at each level of their need.

↳ *My child's school has done some training in attachment, and I'd like to make sure they will work in the ways you're suggesting*

Great. First, find out who trained them, whether it was a taster session or something deeper, which staff were trained and what practical strategies they have implemented as a result of this training. The ideal would be two whole days of Attachment Aware and Trauma Informed training (AATI) for the whole school community. Check they are aware the school needs good foundations in child development, attachment and neuroscience, but that they also need to show evidence of individual planning and an understanding of trauma and loss.

A Pyramid of attachment aware and trauma informed support

Basic attachment awareness greatly complements the work of a school for all children (*see* Level 1 of the Pyramid on p.31), but children who have been traumatised need more than this, hence our development of the model outlined in the **Attachment Aware School Series** with the creation of Team Pupil and the Key Adult relationship, with parents in

The Parent and Carer in School

partnership (Level 2). When the going gets really tough, however, the school will also need to involve external professionals who are experienced in working therapeutically with children who have experienced trauma and loss (Level 3). These children need a very different type of care compared to their peers because of everything they have experienced, culminating in **toxic stress** (*see* p.30). I don't think we should ever underestimate the level of pain many of these children have lived through and are still carrying.

So the piece that's missing all too often in schools for these children, is a knowledge of trauma. Your child has been traumatised in some way, and so will need interventions that support recovery. Such interventions may well be a lifeline in terms of their capacity to function at home, at school and in the wider community. We all have a duty of care to ensure this.

↳ What if my child's school says it can't or won't provide a Key Adult or Team Pupil?

I would first check out whether the school has had any attachment and trauma informed training. Usually schools are doing the best they can with what they know. My guess would be that a school that says this hasn't had this kind of training, so as a starter might be to suggest they check out our Attachment Lead Network website (*see* p.97) for training opportunities or suggest other training providers in this specialist area. Or you could show them what you're reading (especially *Inside I'm Hurting* (2009) and the

Attachment Aware School Series), and say you'd like your child to be supported this way. Sadly, most teacher training doesn't include much on child development, attachment, neuroscience or trauma - yet. The Consortium of Emotional Wellbeing in schools is trying its best to advocate for this! *see* **Useful Contacts**).

Please note that even scarce resources can't excuse a school from providing a stable relationship for your child with an adult in school. I know of one committed school who are struggling a lot financially but who realise that in their catchment area many, many children have developmental vulnerabilities and attachment difficulties and need key adults. Together we came up with the idea of every member of staff employed by the school being allocated a child/children to key work, even the Head and the caretaker! Why not?

Other schools may choose to bring in long term volunteers from charities such as the education charity TLG (Transforming Lives for Good, *see* **Useful Contacts**). Creativity is sometimes needed in the 'how,' but one way or the other we have to pave a way to honour relationship. Schools like the one above know there isn't a choice if they are to reach 'the unreachables' and help them settle. Let's get this Key Adult idea fully embedded into school culture!

But if the school is reluctant, ask if they are willing to invest in relationships that last, and recognise how important this is

The Parent and Carer in School

for pupils who have been wounded 'in relationship', as true at school as much as it is at home. You can tell a lot about a school by who and what they invest in. What are their priorities? What will they do if the going gets tough? Do they have a zero tolerance approach, or are they determined to practice inclusion on every level?

You can play a significant part in raising awareness of the importance of protecting a relationship with an adult in school. And how does this school look after their staff? Do staff have a Key Adult approach? Access to support groups? If not, you may be able to work with the staff to introduce some of these ideas. Ask to hear about a case study of how they supported a child or young person who had experienced significant **relational trauma** and loss. They should now have started logging these for Ofsted. Another strategy would be to encourage the school by letting them know your child's starting point (*see* Factfile in **WAM**) and what you'd find most helpful for your child. Work together with them to put what's needed into place.

Whatever you do, please remember there are many parents out there now with children who have experience of trauma and loss, working with schools with their children in the ways I describe, amazed and delighted with how their child has responded, how much safer and supported they feel, how their learning has progressed. The comments we receive are so moving. We hope you will soon feel the same way.

Part Two

The attachment aware parent and carer and Team Pupil

The whole purpose of Team Pupil is to provide wrap-around care for your child whilst he or she is at school. Here's what you can expect from the different staff in the team:

- From the Key Adult, you can expect a genuine connection for your child, through which he or she can experience safety, regulation, a sense of being known, and joy at regular intervals throughout the school week.

- From the Senior Manager, you will receive an overview and accountability so that you can relax, knowing that your child is receiving the best possible care whilst they are at school.

The Parent and Carer in School

- From your child's Key Teachers, you will notice enhanced interest in what seems to awaken his or her curiosity further, and more feedback on how your child is progressing.

As an adoptive parent, foster carer or guardian, you have many responsibilities in your day-to-day parenting role. The ones I'll highlight opposite are those I will describe in more detail throughout the book, that will help you, alongside Team Pupil, help your child to make the most of everything on offer in school (*for more on each of these areas, please see* pp.34-60).

▷ *How will the school choose the Key Adult for my child?*
We are asking schools to be selective, not just to give these children whoever happens to be around and free! We advocate that children who have experienced relational trauma and loss need Key Adults who are specially chosen to undertake this privileged role within school. Not everyone is suitable. There are special members of staff out there who are robust, who think flexibly and creatively, who want to go the extra mile for children like yours. On my intensive 7 day course we consider designing job descriptions for Key Adults (*and see* **IIH** for more on their role). Making yourself familiar with the whole of the **Attachment Aware Schools Series** will also pave the way for knowing what to expect in terms of each individual's roles and responsibilities within pupil teams.

Responsibilities of parents and carers

- ▷ Provide a rich experiences of closeness, support and fun with you at home and wherever you go
- ▷ Learn how to help your child stay regulated (soothed, relaxed, open and engaged)
- ▷ Highlight how safety, security and stability are created at school
- ▷ Learn to really listen!
- ▷ Support your child to develop a sense of permanency
- ▷ Work alongside Team Pupil to support your child to make the most of school and learning
- ▷ Help your child talk about and share their experiences of school
- ▷ Provide 'buffering' when your child is distressed by the curriculum
- ▷ Learn how to discipline through 'regulation, relationship and reason'
- ▷ Help your child develop pride and confidence in themselves and their abilities
- ▷ Support your child to develop friendships

And last but definitely not least -

- ▷ Look after yourself!

The Parent and Carer in School

10 things Team Pupil say about attachment

When the family are on board it makes such a difference!

I feel like I'm part of the child's extended family as we have worked so closely together over the last 18 months

If I'm honest, I used to keep parents and carers at a bit of a distance, as I suppose I've had some difficult experiences in the past, But now I'm part of Team Pupil I can see that they are so needed and play such a big part in learning

I know I can just pick up the phone and check in about what's happening at home, and together we'll figure out what's really going on!

Consistency at home and school seems to help this pupil not only attend school but have a go at her lessons

I have learnt so much about this pupil because of this family's openness. Without them I would have been working in the dark

aware parents and carers

> We have a laugh every now and then.
> Laughter helps us get through the difficult times.
>
> *As soon as I met the family I realised
> I had lots to offer them and they had lots to
> offer me. I don't think we would have
> been able to hold onto the child I work with without
> all of us working so closely together*
>
> The pupil knows that we all get her,
> that her mum's with us in all this and I
> just think that helps
>
> *I don't think parents and carers realise
> how much of a difference it can make to the pupils
> believing in their potential. Some of our
> pupils have gone on to do all kinds of amazing things
> because their parent believed in them*

The Parent and Carer in School

▷ *Who will Team Pupil call on if they get out of their depth with my child?*

A good enough school will not just carry on regardless, seeking to do everything on their own. Wise members of Team Pupil know that they need to stay connected with external professionals who have specialist skills and expertise, who can carry out assessments, develop individual development plans, provide consultation and supervision, and run support groups or reflective spaces, as the need arises. This is Level 3 of our Pyramid of Support (*see opposite*).

These tasks need to be carried out by those who are therapists or by those who receive regular clinical supervision from therapists, since these children have experienced significant **relational trauma** and loss. Attachment Leads can pave the way by helping schools choose the right kinds of support from as all the services out there. I strongly recommend selecting professionals who have a background in Theraplay® and DDP, specialist trauma interventions that can positively impact recovery especially for those in the fostering and adoption world (*please see* websites for further information, **Useful Contacts**).

As a parent, you can also request external guidance, and work with your child's team to make sure that advice given is followed through.

Attachment aware support for those who are hurting in schools

(drawing on the Seguridad model used by TouchBase™ © theyellowkite.co.uk)

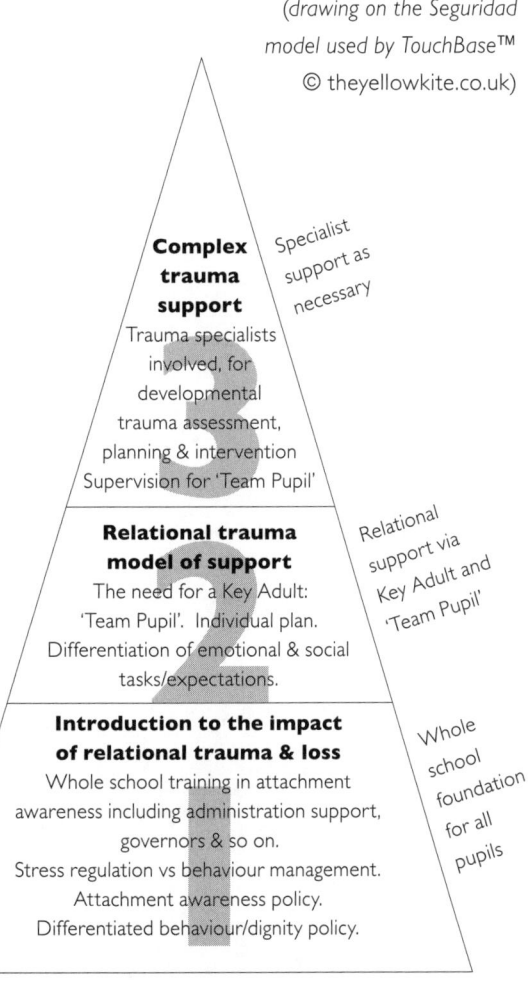

Complex trauma support
Trauma specialists involved, for developmental trauma assessment, planning & intervention
Supervision for 'Team Pupil'

Specialist support as necessary

Relational trauma model of support
The need for a Key Adult: 'Team Pupil'. Individual plan. Differentiation of emotional & social tasks/expectations.

Relational support via Key Adult and 'Team Pupil'

Introduction to the impact of relational trauma & loss
Whole school training in attachment awareness including administration support, governors & so on.
Stress regulation vs behaviour management.
Attachment awareness policy.
Differentiated behaviour/dignity policy.

Whole school foundation for all pupils

The Parent and Carer in School

Part Three

Facilitating the best possible outcome

In this section we'll explore five key aspects of what it means to support your child to fully engage with their school, with Team Pupil and with learning. We'll look at what you can do both at home and when you go into school, what support you can expect and how to find it. We'll also look at how an attachment aware and trauma informed approach can enable your child to grow in self-esteem and confidence, and how to handle stressful times and those moments when discipline becomes necessary. I hope this section will be a rich resource for you and your child as he or she journeys through their education.

The Parent and Carer in School

A ROLES AND RESPONSIBILITIES OF ATTACHMENT AWARE PARENTS AND CARERS

1 Draw your child's attention to what is in place in school that ensures safety, security and stability

You will probably have realised by now that your child really notices when you forget something, when you don't get it quite right for him in terms of a particular response, or when you are too busy or preoccupied to beautifully attune to his needs! Why? Because your child is still viewing the world through a lens of insecurity, based on his past experiences: usually assuming the worst, not the best.

He won't just do this at home but at school as well. So it will be important to gently challenge some of his perceptions as you go along, but only once you have first communicated acceptance of what's happening for him, what he feels. We can't make our children feel anything different to what they feel. We can only offer some other possibilities for them to pick up as and when they feel safe enough to do so. So helping them have what we can think of as 'felt safety' - a real, tangible, internal sense of security - at home and at school - will be crucial. I take my lessons in this from Dr. Dan Hughes, a child and adolescent psychologist of many years' experience, who teaches us to see the world from the child's perspective rather than trying to impose our own. Many of us struggle with simply staying with what our children contribute, rather than moving them on, especially if you are also a teacher like me! But where they are is the starting point towards helping them to experience safety. Feeling understood and 'got' seems to provide that platform.

For example, when a child comes home and says they hate Miss Ore because she is mean and makes them do homework, I wouldn't want to start explaining the benefits of homework! Instead, I'd want to explore the child's anger and her perceptions of Miss Ore. It's likely that she is assuming the worst: that Miss Ore is trying to take something away from her, or at worst setting out to neglect or abuse her.

Yes - you heard rightly - 'neglect' and 'abuse' are the words I chose. I chose them because so many pupils I work with act as if they are being neglected or abused by slight stressors like very ordinary school demands. Things like interrupting screen-time in class, saying a child can't have seconds in the canteen, or when there are not enough pens to go round because the school has run out. All of these can create agitation, stress, rage, humiliation and fear because of a sense of perceived loss in children who have experienced trauma and loss.

Does this ring true for you, from your own experiences with your child or teenager? Their over-reactive responses are 'as

The Parent and Carer in School

if' something terrible has happened or is about to happen? Such responses are common amongst those who have been wounded relationally. So it will be important to first explore their experience of Miss Ore, which is likely to be very different to your own. Exploring in this way will probably bring up other perceptions they've been holding onto that you may not have realised. It is really worth exploring what I call the 'dark cave'! Only when your child feels met - listened to and accepted - will they be in a place to consider anything you might bring to the discussion, so the longer you can stay in their cave the better! I always ask Key Adults in school to 'stay with the uncomfortable feelings for longer than feels comfortable', and the same applies for parents and carers as well.

In this example I might then move into using what I call 'the Hand of Options' (*described more fully in* **WAM**): I'll invite the child to explore some other possibilities with me about Miss Ore's motives and intentions, keeping the focus on the element of doubt. Then after the Hand of Options, I might say something like, "*So with all those possibilities, do you think perhaps we can't know exactly what Miss Ore was thinking when she told you to hand your work in tomorrow?*"

And I might then gently draw attention to what evidence there is for the safety, security and stability the school *is* providing despite this challenge, as these children experience a sense of loss when such things happen. I'll draw attention to what the child can see, feel, hear or touch. Children, like us, are evidence-seeking, so let's point out appropriate things: "*Have you noticed that ... Have you noticed this ...?*" These children are predisposed to seek evidence that confirms their *insecure* view of the world (that everything might be taken away from them, or lost, or things might not be the way they seem). So we will need to work hard to focus on what is in place so that they can begin to recognise and learn about security.

2 Support your child to experience connection with you whilst he or she is at school

Many children who have experienced relational trauma and loss have **developmental vulnerabilities** around permanency - not having a strong sense that you and they are still here, and connected, despite separation. So their experience of school could be an amazing learning opportunity for building connection, in addition to everything they are going to learn relationally and academically there. I don't encourage the use of mobile phones whilst your child is at school, as phones can be very problematic in the school context. I mean providing little stepping stones to help your child hold on. Let me map out some possible ideas of what might support your child to know they are connected to you despite not being able to see you, hear you or sense your presence.

The Parent and Carer in School

- Swap something both ways, for example scarves, to take with you into your separate days
- Make friendship bracelets and swap each time you separate
- Both have the same packed lunch
- Hello and goodbye rituals, for example heart tracing (*please see* **IIH**)
- Put notes in their lunch box
- Enjoy some relational play together and then freeze and take a mental picture for when you are both apart
- Take your child to your workplace and show them your base whilst they are at school, getting them to take a picture of you there that they can keep. You may be permitted to take a picture of your child in their seat, at their table or outside their form room; show them how you keep the picture with you at work or in your wallet or purse
- Using invisible thread - see the lovely children's book about this, *The Invisible String* (Karst 2000)
- Drop off and pick up at a place the child can see from their class window, eg. by the oak tree
- Quick spray of your usual deodorant, perfume or aftershave on their collar
- Both having the same key ring, containing a photograph of both of you together
- A split visual timetable so they know what you are up to whilst they are at school

In addition to these stepping stones, and however strange it may sound, do celebrate the principles of hide-and-seek whenever you can on a regular basis (without teasing) to help your child come to realise that when something is hidden, it still continues to exist. This is so important for them to experience, to help the recovery of their **developmental vulnerability** around permanency. These activities may help.

- Looking at *Where's Wally?* books together
- *Find It* games
- *Hide-and-seek* - hiding in the house, in the garden, behind the car, behind lampposts … but be careful not to raise anxiety by hiding somewhere potentially frightening like a supermarket or other crowded or very open place where your child could easily panic
- Hiding and seeking stones or shells in a tray of sand
- If you're artistic, hide different objects for your child to find, for example by painting a picture with little creatures hiding …

3 Check in with your child about their experiences in school

It's natural to want to chat with your child about how they have experienced their day at school, and important to do so, but not necessarily as soon as you pick them up or they walk through the door! It's a good idea to make sure first of all that they have their basic needs attended to, for example being

The Parent and Carer in School

'watered', fed and possibly offered some kind of physical activity as well, so that they are not met with questions before they're in a more regulated state after the transition from school to home. These are what we might think of as 'regulation needs', which means helping them get back to a basic level of physical comfort and equilibrium. Then ensure you attend to what we can think of as their 'connection needs', essentially, time with you: so that they experience you being alongside them in some way, for example playing together. Only then might you get into chatting about and reflecting on the day together.

Open questions like this may be helpful

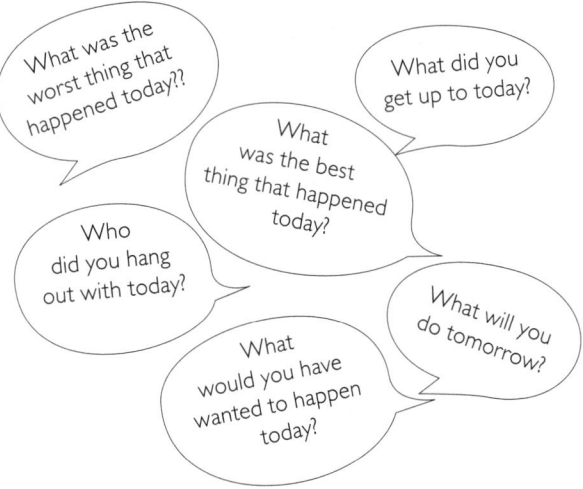

When your child responds, try and work out their feelings from what they say, what they don't say and what you see going on in their body language. Reflect back the possible feelings they may be having. For example, "*Sounds like you felt really angry about that ...*", "*Sounds like you felt quite overwhelmed with that teacher's requests*", "*Sounds like you were really proud when ...*" without any type of judgement, even if you feel that their response is over the top or they have communicated something that doesn't seem accurate (hard for some of us!). Children and teenagers who have experienced relational trauma and loss often don't use feelings words, and equally often feel quite isolated. Communicate that you get what's happening for them. Or at least that you're willing and open to try getting it! So that they gradually get the sense that they are not alone in their story, but understood and joined in with - that you are really there, accepting, curious, empathic and committed to them.

PRACTISE ACTIVE LISTENING

Whatever is going on for your child, please try to ensure you do all you can to listen. This sounds easier than it actually is. Too many of us (myself included!) are inclined to focus on key words, rather than hearing the 'whole' story - the unspoken as well as spoken. We rush in to try and change minds by reassuring, problem-solving and teaching when actually the most powerful communication of all is our presence alongside our children. We have to practise just

The Parent and Carer in School

being rather than *doing*, if we are to enable them to know what it feels like to be still and to use their reflective capacity. Being along someone speaks volumes.

I'm sure you're aware that there can often be a powerful disconnect with many of these children between what they say, what they are feeling inside and what they are communicating through their bodies. Be the one to help them join it all up! Gently reflect out loud on what you notice. For example their eye contact, their tone of voice, their type of voice, the pace of their voice, their tapping, their wriggling, their looking away, their use of distraction …

Be curious … "*I notice that your foot was tapping when we were talking about school. I'm wondering if perhaps you're feeling uncomfortable right now?*" Be a sensory detective, wondering out loud about the possible states, sensations and feelings your child may be experiencing. Don't insist that what you think is the truth of the situation; acknowledge you might get it wrong, and if your child corrects you, simply say something like, "*Oh, OK then*" in an interested and welcoming voice. But don't let that stop you having another go on another occasion, making progress through gentle trial-and-error. It's your willingness to notice, attune, empathise and stay alongside that will count over time, as your child realises you really want to understand her, and she begins to feel safely 'known'. She may also come to understand her own experience, and be better able to express it rather than needing to resort to communicating it through behaviour (*see* Sunderland, 2015 *for many examples*).

4 Help your child regain a calm state following dysregulation

Support your child to be present in the here and now. Do be mindful of when something is getting too much for him. If he is becoming increasingly dysregulated (agitated, aroused, out of control), find a way to reduce the intensity of the activity or the intimacy in some way. For example, get calmer yourself, or a bit more playful if things are too serious, or have a change of face (with someone familiar) or activity. Here are some more suggestions for helping calm to return:

- ☑ Provide rich experiences of being with you through play, whatever your child's age
- ☑ Draw attention to and encourage your child to strengthen his areas of interests, abilities and gifts
- ☑ Use PACE (see p.10)
- ☑ Encourage your child to spend time outside and exercise with him
- ☑ Remain as calm as possible around him
- ☑ Reduce opportunities for shame
- ☑ Reflect back the parts of your child that make him who he is
- ☑ Spend some quality time alone together each week
- ☑ Encourage **relative dependency** for longer than usual (p.13)

The Parent and Carer in School

- ☑ Allow your child some down-time
- ☑ Use structure and predictable routine as much as is possible
- ☑ Draw attention to the fact that as her parent or carer, it's your role to be *bigger, stronger, wiser* and *kinder* (see Circle of Security, p.83).
- ☑ Encourage your child to watch out for and listen in to his body for clues as to how he is doing

DISCIPLINE

Let's reframe discipline and look at the original meaning, which is 'to teach'. With this in mind, please be careful to provide this kind of 'teaching' when your child is in a state that they can hear you, said in a way they can take in. A really helpful and accessible book is *No Drama Discipline* by Daniel Siegel (2105), and I recommend this to schools as well as parents. It is also very important that school takes the lead on repair when there are relationship 'ruptures' at school, and that you take the lead on repair when there are relationship ruptures at home. By relationship rupture, I mean when there has been a conflict or difficulties that have affected your child's relationships with others. So if your child has had problems at school, your role at home will be to merely listen and listen well, as your child will need time and space to process what has happened with you.

When we're thinking about discipline, let's really get to know our own 'shadows' - our own not-so-empathic parts! - that will emerge from time to time from our own backgrounds and stories. Be particularly mindful of what the organisation Circle of Security calls your 'shark music' (*see* the very helpful and accessible clip on their website, circleofsecurity.net).

Like me, you probably don't want anything from the challenges of your own background interfering with the teaching that your individual child needs right now, in this moment. In contrast to what they've experienced before, they need sensitive, attuned, responsive care, not evaluation or angry judgement. We all tend to listen in a more focused way to those we are in close relationship with. Those who have walked life with us, alongside us, have kind of 'earned the right' to gently challenge us, with what some might describe as 'bold love'.

So do everything you can to build connection, deep, quality connection with your child, as *connection* must come first before any kind of *correction*. I think the sequence Dr Bruce Perry (2014) has laid out helps us here:

1 **Regulate** *get sensory, soothing the lower parts of the brain, for example,*
▷ go on the trampoline together
▷ try and both do the plank for as long as possible!
▷ try the 'smell the roses and blow out the candles' breathing technique together (as simple as it sounds!)

The Parent and Carer in School

2 Relate *do some things together that you both enjoy, for example*
- play Jenga together
- blow bubbles and ask child to pop with different body parts (Theraplay®, see **References**)
- go out to the park and play football together

3 Reason *get cognitive, for example,*
- verbal discussion
- explanations, and describing possible reparative opportunities to do together

An example of the Reason stage could include:

i) State calmly in a firm but open way *"There will be no swearing in our house. That stops now. We treat everyone with respect here."*

ii) *"So when we were sitting at the table you felt your brother was looking at you funny. OK, so then you poked him and you didn't feel that made any difference. Then you got up and slammed out of the room. Wow, you were so angry with your brother for looking at you funny, I can really understand that if you thought he was laughing at you, it would have been really hard …"* Then you can move into exploring what happened further, maybe even using the Hand of Options (see **WAM**)

iii) *"OK, the lounge is in a right state after all that upset earlier. We could clear it up together, or we could time how long Mum takes to clear it up and then make up the time for her by doing something like cook something for everyone for dinner, to make up for it. What do you reckon?"*

Whenever something has gone wrong and needs to be attended to, please use this sequence of the 3 R's listed in the order described (it is also good to use this sequence in ordinary, everyday interactions too!). In this way we respect biology and give our children the best possible opportunity to learn from whatever we need to teach them. A lot of us have a belief system that states we must deal with any conflicts or relationship ruptures immediately, but unfortunately that belief system doesn't take our biology into account. Sometimes it's best to wait. We do need to respond, but when we reckon the time is right.

Remember that *when things get tough, our children need us the most*, so this is not the time to pull ourselves away or distance ourselves from them, for example by ignoring them or putting them in 'time out'. They need you to be nearby. They need your proximity, but not so close that they feel trapped or claustrophobic. They need your presence. Your availability and openness. They need your thinking. They need an exit strategy, because more often than not they don't have one and are so flooded by emotion they are in no place to think straight at all!

The Parent and Carer in School

There will be times when we all mess up: when we kick ourselves for not having used our own thinking brain, those times when our limbic system (a more primitive part of our brain) seems to override our reflective capacity (the most sophisticated part) and we get really emotional and intense ourselves. I'm sure we have all been there! At those times, be humble and admit you have got it wrong. Model apology. Model finding an exit strategy. There will be times when we may have exacerbated a difficult situation, and at those times we may even want to step back physically and use a surrender action. I was so impressed when I heard of an assistant head, retreating and doing this with a "*Whoaaaa!*" He was taken aback himself by the response from the pupil, who just couldn't believe that a senior teacher could be so open and vulnerable.

That boy saw a gentle strength that day, something that had been missing from his own father who had abused his strength and power. Ask for another go. Be willing to show how to re-engage.

5   Work alongside Team Pupil to support your child in school

Support your child to reach their potential in school, and welcome the creation of Team Pupil (*see below for much more on this* p.64), or see if you can encourage the school to appoint a Key Adult and Team Pupil if your school hasn't yet got this system in place (*see* p.22 above).

6 Engage your child's interest and curiosity in what is being taught at school

Education is such an amazing privilege and opportunity. We don't want your child to miss out on any of the experiences on offer. Your child needs to know that you value the importance of education, of using your own exploratory system, so model interest and curiosity yourself. Your child will be influenced significantly by your attitude to education, so take an active interest in what is being covered at school. If you don't know already (it can be hard to keep up), ask the teacher/s for a 'map' of what will be covered over the next half-term or term, so that you are one step ahead.

When you're out and about, draw your child's attention to anything that might be relevant. Join the library and help them access books, magazines and journals, not just the internet - gradually offer a broader horizon. Model how to be a bit of a detective, and how exciting curiosity and exploration can be, because your child may find this extremely difficult and challenging. Plan trips to visit places that might open up further learning opportunities like parks, farms, theatres, museums and galleries.

Engage their exploratory system by providing multi-sensory learning opportunities, encouraging exploration through all their senses. Be wary of using 'don't touch' commands unless there is a sign for the public stating this! Many of these children need to touch and smell things in order to make

The Parent and Carer in School

sense of all the information they are attempting to process. And it's a way to help your child bring all their faculties together and help their development, with you alongside.

7 Provide the 'buffering' needed when the curriculum touches your child personally

From time to time activities, topics, books, films, plays and lessons will trigger painful or uncomfortable feelings for your child. Whenever possible, be prepared. It's important that you know your child's story well ... do create a Factfile (**WAM**) together with your social worker (if you have one), to revisit from time to time, so you can consider possible areas that might well be stress triggers for your child. Find out about the curriculum map for the half-term or term (*as recommended above*) by liaising with your child's Team Pupil who can co-ordinate this for you.

Please note that your child won't need to be taken out of classes where something which might trigger memories or associations for them will be discussed, but they will need preparation time together with you privately first.

It may be that your child will also need opportunity to rehearse what he or she feels willing to contribute more publicly in the classroom context on the subject about to be discussed. They will also need your support to know how much to share about themselves in other places and with other people.

Some children and teenagers share everything all in one go and leave themselves feeling very exposed and vulnerable. Others won't share anything, and hide their story as if it's something to be ashamed of. So it will be important to liaise with the Key Adult from Team Pupil to consider your child's hidden needs, as they may well present very differently in the context of school, and it's so important that everyone works together on this.

Your child may have often experienced deep feelings of powerlessness, so it is even more essential that we explain that now, she has choices. I often use W.I.S.E Up! - an American tool (*see* **References**) designed to help those adopted internationally, which can also be used in domestic context. The choices (which I have further developed) are:

W WALK AWAY
It is your business. You do not need to say anything. Just keep it to yourself. No-one needs to know that what has happened has affected you at all.

▌ SAY *"IT'S PRIVATE"*
By saying this you let the other person know that something has affected you, but you are communicating that you don't want to talk about it.

The Parent and Carer in School

S SHARE SOMETHING
Don't say everything about how it has affected you, but maybe just share one or two aspects.

E EDUCATE
Use the opportunity to educate others. So many people don't understand how relational trauma and loss affect children and young people: so maybe this is your moment?

Learning about the brain

As a parents or carer, you may find it helpful to keep yourself updated on the latest research on the nervous system so that you can better understand what is going on, use appropriate practical strategies and pass on helpful pointers to your children. Better self-awareness leads to self-control, and that's true for all of us! There are some great books out there, so no need to be daunted: *Help! I've Got an Alarm Bell Going off in My Head!* by Louisa Aspden (2015) is a good one for your child or teenager, or you could read it together. Do check out Daniel Siegel's books *The Whole-Brain Child* (2012) and *No Drama Discipline* (2015) too. Also have a look at The Hand Model of the Brain - a Youtube clip by Daniel Siegel (*see* **References**) and Bruce Perry's website (*see* **Useful Contacts**).

8 Support your child to be proud of who they are

Draw attention to public figures who have had difficult starts, especially those who have achieved a lot in the world in leadership and creativity, for example, Abraham Lincoln and Maya Angelou. Support your child to realise that their vulnerabilities can one day become an area of strength. Do take time to check out a beautiful Japanese art form called Kintsugi pottery on Youtube (*see* **References**). Kintsugi is treasured pottery that has been broken and put back together again with special powdered gold glue. So the cracks become the key feature of the pottery. This really resonates in the work I do, in which vulnerabilities tend to become a person's strengths.

Things like this can help you and your child consider the beauty and hope that is possible during the restoration process after suffering relational trauma and loss: many treasures can be picked up along the way. Perhaps this is especially important for us all to think about in the West, where 'perfection' seems to be held out as the only way to be - these days there is a huge amount of pressure on young people, especially from the internet and social media, to live up to certain supposed 'ideals'. This way of thinking can be very costly physically and psychologically, particularly to those who have experienced relational disruption.

Do also consider together with your child the possibility

The Parent and Carer in School

of living a life so well so that they defy all expectations of themselves and others. I love the story of the Agave plant that was lying dormant for 40 years until one day it grew 35 foot within three months and burst through the roof of the greenhouse, much to everyone's amazement! Your children could well be late bloomers, and my, there are so many possibilities. Remember that everything you invest now emotionally, mentally and physically will make an enormous difference!

Get your child to learn about the bumble bee. Did you know that bumble bees shouldn't really be able to fly? But they do - they defy physics. No-one told them they couldn't fly: they discovered their wings and just started using them. Support your child to know they don't have to be bound by the past, that they are free to be who they were intended to be first time round. Have high expectations and watch them fly!

9 Supporting your child to develop and maintain friendships

Make opportunities for your child to have time with their peers at home, at others' homes and out and about in public spaces. Make sure they get a rich diet of experiences and different settings.

▷ Stay close by
▷ Supervise
▷ Set up play dates /meetings outside home in a neutral space
▷ Structure free time
▷ Ensure your child gets the opportunity to settle/regulate through some kind of physical exercise before and during time together with a friend
▷ When things go wrong between your child and a friend, listen and accept their perspective, even if you consider it to be distorted. Then use the Hand of Options (see above)
▷ Encourage your child to find out three new things about their friend each time they meet up!

TIME ONLINE - KEEPING YOUR CHILD SAFE

Most children and adolescents spend time online nowadays. However, I've noted that the pupils I oversee spend even more time online than their peers, if they are allowed to follow their own wishes! I think we need to be very mindful of this, especially as these particular pupils have real vulnerability

The Parent and Carer in School

around relationship. They have been wounded within relationship and so relationship needs to be the vehicle for adaption and recovery: not a virtual relationship which can distort the child's perspective further, but a real life one!

However, that said, social media can offer a helpful stepping-stone to supporting those children and adolescents who feel 'lost from mind' and who are struggling with permanency. A text or a message can sometimes bridge the gap that can feel like a black hole to those who are hurting inside. With all of this, moderation is key. It will be important that you oversee time being spent online, what they are up to and who they are liaising with.

I must acknowledge that I am especially concerned by those who have dissociative tendencies, those children with an already fragmented sense of self who distance themselves as a default position at times of stress and overwhelm. We need to support children such as these to reduce screen-time and become more physically active so that they can be grounded and connected. I worry about those who disconnect further. When minds and bodies are disconnected, anything is possible! Surely our joint role is to support these children to be integrated little beings. A helpful book for those considering the use of IT is *Toxic Childhood* by Sue Palmer (2007); the latest edition includes information on this very topic.

Obviously for children in care or adopted there are further concerns about the possibility of contact with those they need supervision around, for example birth families, and the possibility of predatory others out there who groom children. For this reason, our children need support in knowing how to keep themselves safe online. We can do all we can as parents and carers but even better if the children themselves realise their own boundaries. CEOP (Child Exploitation and Online Protection Centre) offer fantastic online resources and clips that are suitable for all ages. Please do check out their website ceop.police. uk/. I particularly like what they have produced on what to consider when publishing any private material, as so many children (and adults) do not appreciate the possibility of many, many strangers out there accessing and viewing very personal information via text, pictures and video.

10 Self care - looking after you

When I'm thinking about being alongside traumatised children, I find it helpful to remember the advice given on planes; put your own oxygen mask on first before helping others. The same is true for therapeutic parenting and support in school. It's really important that you prepare yourself for the long haul by having a self-care plan in place. It's also really important to be explicit about and model for your child how to manage stress. Have a think about who you could reach out to and connect with on a weekly, monthly, half-termly, termly and yearly basis, to help you with this.

The Parent and Carer in School

Think what you can do with the answers to the questions below on a weekly basis:

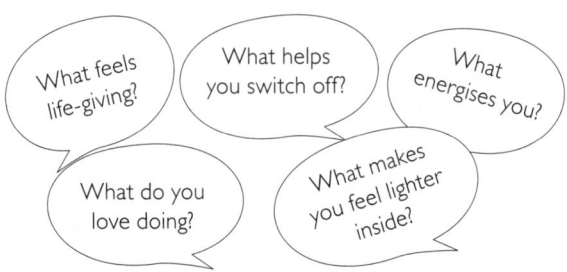

BLOCKED CARE AND BLOCKED TRUST

Many of these children present adults with behaviours that show their distrust in us. Many have experienced the betrayal of intimacy at the hands of their birth parents. They have learned to be pseudo-independent. However, when you are on the receiving end of this *blocked trust* (Hughes 2016) it can be excruciating, especially when you feel like you are attempting to pour so much of your time, energy, patience, care and love into them. Sometimes they seem completely oblivious. Other times they act like they hate you. If you're on the receiving end of this, time and time again, it's no wonder your own systems begin saying enough is enough, and eventually start closing off your usual patience and care.

This is what Hughes & Baylin have called *blocked care* (2012). I've worked alongside parents who have been really distressed by their own apparent lack of caring feelings after many years of trying to reach their unresponsive child. These are parents and carers who are even contemplating the possibility of a placement breakdown, of the child leaving, much as they never wanted that to happen. As soon as they understand the science behind this, that it is a change in their brains and not any lack of love or care on their own part, they realise that they're not alone, and they can begin the journey towards recovery. Just as the rest of Team Pupil know that being connected ourselves, experiencing each other's presence, attention, attunement and responsiveness, can unlock our own capacity for care again. We all need to have an experience from that deep well of empathy in order to be able to empathise again. If you are concerned by this about yourself then please do make contact with a therapist who has been trained in DDP who will be able to support you in

The Parent and Carer in School

this (*see* references for DDP therapist list on DDP webpages). It can take time to unblock care. You may fear that you will never be 'you' again, but you will, I promise. Seasons come and seasons go. Nothing ever remains the same.

To build up awareness that can lead to a deeper understanding and more creative ideas for parenting your children, please do have a go at these exercises.

> **EXERCISE 1**
> LET'S CONSIDER OUR OWN EXPERIENCES OF SCHOOL:
> - What comes to mind for you when someone says the word 'school'?
> - What were you top three memories at school?
> - What would you like to forget?
> - Identify anything that helped you at school.
> - Identify anything that hindered you at school.
> - Did you work hard at school? Why? Why not?
> - Did you feel that your teachers realised your strengths?
> - What makes you believe that, if they did? If they didn't, why do you think they missed them?
> - How did you manage homework?
> - How might this awareness affect how you support your child now?

EXERCISE 2
LET'S CONSIDER OUR OWN EXPERIENCES OF FAMILY:

- What comes to mind when someone says the word 'family'?
- Do you have any happy memories of growing up?
- Do you have any sadness about your childhood?
- Did you feel close to your parents? If you did - what helped? If not - what got in the way?
- Did you play much? Do you play now?
- How was conflict handled in your home?
- Did you ever see your parents stressed? If so, how did that impact you?
- If not, what techniques for managing stress did you observe?
- What helped you feel safe at home?
- What unsettled you at home?
- Did your parents support you in your education? If they did, how did they do that? If not, what would you have liked?
- How might this awareness support you with your child at home?

The Parent and Carer in School

EXERCISE 3
LET'S EXPLORE HOW WE MANAGE REGULATION:
- When the going gets tough, what do you usually do?
- How does stress manifest itself in you?
- How would someone know you were stressed? How do you know?
- Do you do anything to prevent a build-up of stress? What works best?
- What do you do when you feel highly stressed? What works best?
- How regulated are you on an average day?
- What are your stress triggers?
- What are your calmers?
- How might you use this awareness to help your child learn to self-regulate?

EXERCISE 4
LET'S EXPLORE OUR RELATIONSHIPS:
- Who would you consider to be part of your support network?
- Who would you count on if there was a big crisis? What would they do that helps?

- Who do you have fun with?
- How do you determine whether someone is trustworthy or not?
- How can you use this awareness to help your child build relationships face-to-face and online?

EXERCISE 5
LET'S EXPLORE REASON:
- If you need to focus, what helps?
- When do you think most clearly?
- How and when do you problem-solve?
- If you needed to make a big decision, would you connect with anyone?
- How did you do at school?
- How would you describe yourself as a learner?
- When do you feel most curious? Most excited about learning?
- How can you use this awareness to help your child develop openness to learning?

The Parent and Carer in School

B WORK ALONGSIDE TEAM PUPIL TO SUPPORT YOUR CHILD IN SCHOOL

We so need you on board alongside Team Pupil in school. Don't let anyone or anything dissuade you! These children need a joined up, integrative approach, and who better to give them this than those who know them best at home and those who know them best at school. Your contributions really matter!

Supporting your child in their day-to-day life in school

- ▷ Support your child to pack their bag for school
- ▷ Support your child to get to and from school
- ▷ Support your child to arrive at school as calm and regulated as possible
- ▷ When you're away from home whilst your child is at school, swap 'transitional objects' (*things that promote feelings of connection see* p.38)
- ▷ Support your child to complete homework or coursework
- ▷ Support good personal hygiene
- ▷ Encourage connection with other children and other adults known to your family through school
- ▷ Attend Parents' Evenings
- ▷ Attend any special assemblies, sports days or performances your child is in (*and see* p.73)

- ▷ Photo journal your child's journey through education so they can remember and re-visit everything they have achieved
- ▷ Show interest in everything your child is doing at school
- ▷ Encourage reading by having all kinds of reading material out and about, by reading yourself and by reading to your child and listening to them read. Make it fun! And join your local library.
- ▷ Visit places of educational interest
- ▷ Boundary screen time
- ▷ Boundary access to sweet and carbohydrate foods
- ▷ Give child a varied, healthy diet at home and in their snack box for school
- ▷ Refer to the picture of Team Pupil in a positive way whenever you can, reminding your child of these adults who are all keeping him or her in mind
- ▷ Be seen smiling and laughing together with different members of the team. Your child needs to know you get on!

Working with your child's Team

- ▷ Flag up with the school that your child is fostered, adopted or on a special guardianship
- ▷ Write up a Factfile for the school (**WAM**) so they know your child's starting point. Empathy is necessary in support work in school

The Parent and Carer in School

▷ Ensure you know who the staff in Team Pupil are. Meet with them all once, preferably together

▷ Complete the home school review sheet at the weekend about the previous week at home. Be as honest as possible

▷ Check in with the Key Adult on a weekly basis using the home school prompt sheet (**IIH**)

▷ If school send home material that might trigger your child, please go through it together with your child first so that he has some preparation time (see p.50)

▷ Trust those supporting your child and allow them to do what they think they need to do

▷ If anything comes up that might dysregulate your child, for example contact or holidays and so on, do let Team Pupil know with plenty of notice

Working at your child's school

Please may I strongly recommend that you do not work in the same school if your child is developmentally vulnerable? If you are already doing this, please don't feel judged, I know you've been doing your absolute best with what you know: I am simply sharing this recommendation based on my experience over the last 16 years in schools. I've observed how having an adoptive parent or foster mum or dad in school can lead to complex dynamics around envy, as the child can see their parent getting alongside and close to other pupils and often misinterprets what this is about. Your child needs to receive the message that you are their parent or carer, loud and clear. In effect, they need to be claimed as yours, and claimed again and again and again! You can't revisit this enough. Claiming is a process, not a discrete event.

I know this will go against the grain of what schools usually request with regards to parent helpers, but please just hold your ground and explain that this type of support will not be appropriate for your relationship with your child at home and in the context of the class.

Home School partnership

Do resist the temptation to live at the school! Make as much time as you can for a quality goodbye to your child, and then hand your child over to Team Pupil. This will require *trust*, so ensure you know who Team Pupil are by requesting a face-to-face meeting and sharing your child's Factfile with them (*see* **WAM**). Ask to see your child's individual development plan from time to time and think with Team Pupil about how funding is being used to support him or her (and indeed others who have experienced relational trauma and loss). This accountability will always be important and your interest can really make a difference. Equally, letting go while your child is at school will be needed.

I hope that over time, Team Pupil will prove to you that they are trustworthy with your child. The majority of the education staff I have worked with are dedicated

The Parent and Carer in School

professionals who have entered the profession because they want to make a difference in the lives of children. With the right training and access to the latest information, they can make a profound impact on your child's life both relationally and academically.

Do support the use of the home school review prompt sheets (*outlined in* **IIH**). I encourage the Key Adult to complete this as the main co-ordinator of your child's individual support in school. The Key Adult will know your child's individual stressors and calmers in the school context through the ongoing process of building relationship with him or her. In secondary it will be assumed that subject teachers will liaise with Team Pupil if there is a problem: so no news should be viewed as good news! So school completes the sheet on a

10 pieces of advice for parents from parents

Get into school sooner rather than later. Partnership makes all the difference.

Sometimes you just have to let go and trust the process. I think this is hard when you care so much, but it has to be done.

Don't hold back on your child's story. The staff need to know. The more they know the more they will 'get' your child.

Friday afternoon and emails it on to you to avoid these sheets being lost in transit (which might create another possibility for further shame for your child).

Do complete the template yourself based on what you have experienced together with your child and send onto the school, so they have it by Monday morning. Please ensure you share any stressors or calmers you've noticed happening at home; some parents simply write about school third hand! That's not what's wanted. It's about both parties - home and school - keeping the other informed. These templates are most effective when both parties share as much as they have experienced in their own contexts. We each hold a piece of the puzzle and together we can help these children figure out who they are.

> *It can be nerve-wracking going into school meetings so take someone with you, your partner, a friend or someone like the parent partnership officer from the council, at least 'til you find your feet.*
>
> *It can be really frustrating that education staff haven't had training in this area but bite your lip and remember they are doing their best.*
> **Be patient!**

The Parent and Carer in School

If education staff tell you that there isn't enough funding for Key Adults just smile, and ask whether much additional funding is actually needed when a healthy relationship with a Key Adult in school is your main concern: a protected relationship that lasts over time.

Don't bombard the school with too much information in one go. Give them info over time as it is more likely to go in.

If you don't understand the education lingo you are not alone! Slow staff down and get them to explain as they are not always aware that we don't know what they mean.

If staff are concerned by what the other children might think about your child being treated differently, try looking confused and state that you would have hoped that all the children were treated differently as they are all so different, aren't they? Explain that you don't treat siblings the same.

C STRESSORS AND CALMERS

Following on from the Factfile that you have shared with Team Pupil in your child's school, it will be important to continue noticing what stresses and calms your child. Have a look at the States Continuum created by Dr Bruce Perry remembering that children who have experienced trauma and loss are already in a state of alarm because of all the toxic stress they experienced in the past. We need to notice what state they are in on our watch, whilst we're with them, and respond accordingly to help them stay in or regain the best state possible.

Cognitive state	Abstract	Concrete	Emotional	Reactive	Reflexive
Internal state	Calm	Alert	Alarm	Fear	Terror

From Perry, 2003

Are they at the low end of alarm, maybe even in a state of calm or alert? If so, what seemed to support this? Are they moving across the states continuum into fear or terror? If so, what seemed to precipitate this? We won't be able to get to the bottom of everything, so don't give yourself a hard time. Some triggers are internal. However, as you know your child well you will be able to make good guesses based

The Parent and Carer in School

on your attunement to him or her. Remember behaviour is communication, so every now and then consider what your child might be trying to say if she could express her needs in words. This is such a significant part of therapeutic parenting and support in school.

We will pick up many clues to help guide us, and we need to see ourselves as both translators (of the clues) and stress regulators. Too many parenting programmes rely very heavily on stickers, certificates and other rewards, when our children have faulty nervous systems that trigger at the slightest stressors*. When we understand that our children are merely responding to a faulty 'alarm' going off, we realise that rather than them needing our discipline, or lectures, they need our help to support their bodies and minds to catch up with the reality of the here and now. Easier said than done, I know! However, this has to be where we begin. Some children will look like they are merely being naughty; but hang on a moment and you'll see that there's so much more going on than initially meets the eye. We need to help tame their faulty alarm systems.

So the clues we pick up will help guide us in choosing state dependent interventions (*see* the chart above and the approach on p.45) rather than relying on behaviorist

*What we advocate is that parents have access to theraputic parenting programmes such as those based on Golding 2007, because they complement the **Attachment Aware School Series** *model of support.*

strategies (reward and punishment) that are too simplistic and don't match the complexities of these children. Each child has their own unique story and we need to learn their story through relationship with them. The files and what you've been told by social workers and others about your child's past will never be sufficient: they are merely our starting point. What your children have lived through will actually only become clearer the longer you live with them.

You might like to create Calm boxes and bags at home with your child, and let the school know what things from the box or bag works best. Calm boxes, bags and purses carry a range of two or three minute activites to help up- or down-regulate whoever's box or bag it is - our children or ourselves (*and see* **IIH**). Let's model regulation!

Planning for special occasions

Co-modelling calm at times of stress, for example when your child is entering a race or performing in assembly, can be very helpful. Be mindful at these times that they need to see you grounded and not too over-excited, so they can understand how you maintain that state; and they need strategies for how to stay calm and grounded themselves. Focus on the effort and process rather than the outcome of competition or performance. These children need support knowing it is good to join in, to belong, to contribute, to have a go, because they are valued and they matter. Don't get too caught up in the achievement side of things if possible, but do notice out loud anything you can see they are getting better at or are good at. Many of the pupils I work with can go into overwhelm when praised, so just keep it matter-of-fact, and move on. Try and focus more on the person they are becoming, rather than what they do!

D MAPPING PROGRESS

There is a lot of pressure on schools nowadays to prove their worth through their SATS and GCSE outcomes. We need to support everyone in education who is working hard at ensuring these children have the same quality educative opportunities as their peers. However, we also need to support them to realise that these children usually have spikey profiles because of everything they have experienced and are experiencing now. Internal and external trauma triggers, contact, losses and stressors in their present everyday life will all come into play at some point.

So it will be important for all of us to think about the child or children we parent or care for throughout their educational journeys, as their needs will change from day to day and over time. There will be times when nurture will need to be increased and challenge decreased. There will be times when challenge needs to be increased and nurture decreased, and you can work with Team Pupil to help everyone develop sensitivity to what is needed when.

So for example - Ciara has just had some very unsettling news that her birth mother has gone into rehab again. This news has shaken her up and she has become more clingy, more irritable and preoccupied. Her adoptive mum phones school to get a message to the Key Adult to pass on to Team Ciara this week. She explains the situation, and recommends they all decrease challenge this week and increase Ciara's nurture, for example, allowing increased time in her safe space, not being expected to do homework, being allowed to check in with the inclusion department and have some space away from the usual demands of school life if necessary. Once she is stabilised though, she can return to her usual routine and functioning.

E TRANSITION PLANNING AND PREPARATION

Your child may find all kinds of transition challenging, both at and away from home. Here are some examples you might find familiar from what happens in school:

- ☺ Darren finds it hard when he has to find where his next class is on his own
- ☺ Chantal gets agitated when the teacher tells the class to stop and put their books away
- ☺ Rosa goes very quiet when anyone talks about leaving and going to her next school
- ☹ Liza starts becoming confrontational at the end

The Parent and Carer in School

of a school year when her anxiety increases
- ☺ Lee lies down in the corridor when it's time for lesson changes
- ☺ Sandeep climbs the nearest tree when he is asked to write up his experiment
- ☺ Your child … ?

In my book, *What About Me?* (2011) I give many more examples in both primary and secondary, and for the move in between, and many practical suggestions for how you and the school can help. But here's a quick list to check out when you know a transition is coming up.

Don't...

- Get into a control battle
- Rush your child on
- Be sarcastic
- Square up to them
- Join in with the drama
- Lose your cool!
- Respond in an equally hostile or anxious way
- Be matter-of-fact
- Overlook their distress
- Leave them behind
- Shame them
- Isolate, seclude or exclude!

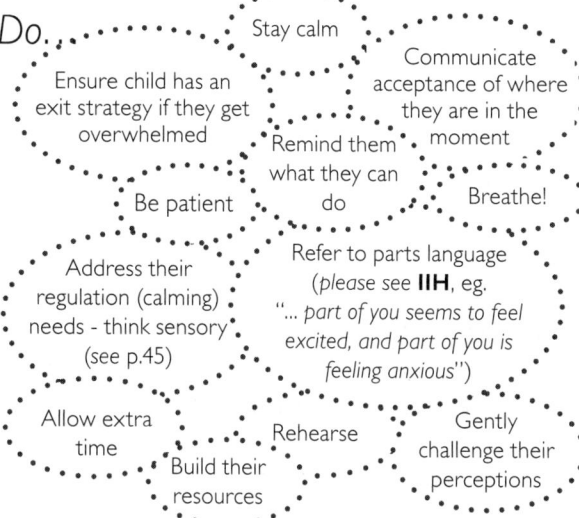

Finally

Let's go forward together, determined to support our children with their muddles. Let's do all we can to build community rather than division, as we don't want anyone isolated along the way: it isn't good for anyone's health or wellbeing, and definitely won't be helpful for your children, our pupils. Be the listening ears at home, but remember these children need a careful balance of both nurture and gentle challenge so connect first, communicate acceptance and then offer some other possibilities that your child can either pick up or leave. Lend them your pre-frontal cortex from time to time! - in other words, your thinking brain, remembering their developmental vulnerabilities.

The Parent and Carer in School

Respectful nurturing parenting will eventually make an impact. Surprise these children with your flexibility and creative responses to things that seem overwhelming for them. Work with Team Pupil to make school a safe, secure and stable place where your child can learn to trust adults outside the family and make the most of everything on offer in education.

There will be challenges. There's a lot for us all to learn and remember. But most of all, remember you are doing a fabulous job, even when you don't feel it. As child and adolescent psychologist Kim Golding advised,

> Helping a child overcome their fear of connection with others, based on their past hurtful experience … is probably one of the hardest tasks we can ask anyone to do, whether educator or parent. For parents, however, this is the biggest ask. Children hurt by adults in their earliest years, need to learn safety with parents. This then provides them with a secure base to move forward and make the most of everything the world offers.
> *(personal communication, 2016)*

And this is true too for what you as a parent can help your child find in school. With the 'big ask' Kim describes in mind, please go steady but surely with your children. They will get there, but they need all our collective patience and relentless care alongside them, as long as it takes.

10 things children and teenagers say about their parent or carer working with Team Pupil

I used to think there was no point to school but since I lived with * and * they've made me see differently.

I used to phone my mum all the time at school 'cos I didn't want to be there, but now I can't remember the last time I called her!

My mum says my team know what they are doing. This makes me feel OK.

I know that they stick up for me whenever I need help.

He had to put up with a lot when I first moved in but I know they mean it now.

I don't always get good grades but I know my mum just wants me to try my best.

I used to have bad self-esteem but since * cared for me I feel OK about being me.

They feel like kinda friends I suppose.

It's good having carers back at home who believe in you.

I can see mum and dad get on with my team. They are always laughing.

The Parent and Carer in School

Glossary

Additional attachment figure This is the person selected in school to get alongside a child with attachment difficulties, here described as the **Key Adult**. This person could be a teaching/learning assistant or teacher, or mentor. The task is to relate to the child using strategies derived from attachment and developmental principles. Their aim is to create a relationship which will facilitate opportunities for second chance learning, so that the child can have the experience of making healthier attachments than previously. These experiences encourage the development of neural connections in the brain, which in turn leads to the development of conscience, cause-and-effect thinking, logic and empathy.

Attachment history A child's history of significant relationships and the security, or lack of security, safety, or lack of safety, of those relationships with parents, wider family, carers or adopters. It may also include other significant individuals including teachers or even pets. Any type of trauma and loss is especially important to note, even if a loss had been deemed to be in the best interest of the child (for example, loss of contact with an abusive parent): as is any kind

The Parent and Carer in School

of extraordinary stress experienced. We need to know what they have lived through from pregnancy onwards, if there has been any kind of potential disruption to the usual bonding/attachment process.

Attachment Lead An Attachment Lead is an appointed and trained member of staff in the school who seeks to lead the way in attachment awareness and trauma informed interventions and embed them into policy on behalf of troubled pupils. This is usually a member of support staff on the ground leading through practice with individual pupils, and a member of Senior Management leading through advocacy and strategic action amongst the whole school community. See www.attachmentleadnetwork.net for more information on the training required.

Attachment system An innate urge within humans (and other mammals) that impels us to seek promixity to and relationship with others. Attachment serves two important functions: a protective function and a secure base effect. It is in our interest to stay close to another person, especially when we are very young, defenceless and vulnerable. Staying close can keep us safe. It is also in our interest to have someone to act as our **secure base**. If we have a secure base, we are then freed up to set off out of our comfort zone into the unfamiliar, the unknown, into unchartered territory - the world is ours to be curious and learn about. We can do this knowing that we can return to our secure base before venturing off again.

Our secure base gives us the confidence we need in order to take the risks required in learning. Our attachment system (of neural connections and hormone release leading to attachment seeking behaviour) is activated if we experience anxiety.

Blocked care According to Hughes & Baylin (2012), when a child or adolescent continually rejects care and nurture from an adult, the brain systems that support empathy within the adult begin to close down as a protective response. The adult can feel frustrated, irritated, hopeless, rejecting or numb. They may continue to provide care, from a position of 'duty', but find it difficult or impossible to relate to the child from the loving and open engaged stance necessary for authentic and healing relationship (**STL** p.324).

Circle of Security® The Circle of Security® is a relationship based early intervention programme designed to enhance attachment security between parents and children. Decades of university-based research have confirmed that secure children exhibit increased empathy, greater self-esteem, better relationships with parents and peers, enhanced school readiness, and an increased capacity to handle emotions more effectively when compared with children who are not secure. The Circle of Security® intervention and the graphic designed around it are intended to help caregivers increase their awareness of their children's needs and whether their own responses meet those needs. With increased awareness, parents can expand their moment-to-moment parenting

The Parent and Carer in School

choices where needed. In this shift from mind-blindness to seeing what is hidden in plain sight lies the potential to break the stranglehold of problematic attachment patterns, passed from one generation to the next, that can compromise healthy relationships throughout a child's life span. (*With thanks to Jenny Peters and Glen Cooper*)

Containment When a baby is distressed or dysregulated, she needs repeated experiences of her parent or carer being 'bigger, stronger, wiser and kinder' (**Circle of Security®**) to help to 'hold' her feelings and experience and make sense of what is happening, until she is able to do this for herself. Similarly, adult individuals and teams need **Senior Managers** who can create containing environments to support their work containing children who have experienced relational trauma.

Developmental Trauma A term used by Van der Kolk (2014) and many other attachment aware and trauma informed practitioners to describe a child's experiences of repeated or prolonged trauma through neglect, abuse, abandonment, violence, loss, parental substance misuse or addiction. Developmental trauma implies that the child's developing brain will have been impacted, with negative effects on the development of their executive functions, motor skills, and capacity to self-regulate, communicate and relate. Left unattended at home and/or in school, the effects of developmental trauma are likely to persist into adulthood and have profound effects on every aspect of the individual's life.

Disrupted relationships/connections Relationships and connections that have been disrupted or compromised for the individual child through having early experiences of loss, abuse, neglect, trauma, domestic violence, or parental substance abuse or mental ill health. Disruption isn't necessarily intentional (although it can be) but can come about due to circumstance: for example, medical complications at birth, having a mother who becomes unwell after birth … the ordinary development of brain connections may have been disrupted if these experiences happen at certain crucial times, or for prolonged periods. Disruptions often compromise or disrupt trust. There are many children in our care who have experienced intimacy betrayals at the hands of their own birth parents. The deep distrust that has been created out of relational experience is then often projected onto other adults, regardless of their intentions or motives. We can in fact get caught up in their time-warp, experiencing the distress, grief and rage intended for someone else, in another time and place.

Exploratory system An innate urge within humans (and other mammals) that impels us to explore, experiment, play, and thereby learn. The exploratory system (of neural connections and hormone release leading to exploratory behaviour) is activated or reaches its full potential when the attachment system is well attended to. If the attachment system is not attended to, the exploratory system (which is needed for learning) will be impeded by ongoing anxiety.

The Parent and Carer in School

Hypervigilance A subliminal rapid-reaction mammalian defence developed in response to repeated or continual traumatic experience. The individual becomes wired for a state of high alert at all times to any potential danger in the environment, thus 'primed for threat'. He or she may view or interpret events, words or actions as dangerous which others around them view as innocent or innocuous.

Insecure attachment This indicates a level of insecurity that interferes with the child's ability to relate in a healthy or appropriate way to other people. Such insecurity arose from early uncertainties about the reliability of his or her parent or primary carer. We can observe too much dependence or too much independence in his response to his needs and the satisfaction of those needs. There are traditionally three main types of insecure attachment, sometimes described as avoidant, ambivalent and disorganised.

Primary Attachment Figure This is the person who takes the main caring/parenting role for the child at home. It could be a parent, grandparent, foster carer, adoptive parent, kinship carer or residential children's worker. The person is someone on whom the child is dependent for many needs including safety, and for being able to develop in all ways, including the ability to make and maintain relationships. The experience that a child has with his primary attachment figure will shape his view of himself, others and the world around him.

Regulatory system If we have received consistent and sufficient regulatory experiences ourselves, through being attuned to and received by calming and soothing others, especially in our early years, then we are more able to internalise what becomes our own regulatory system (internal and external tools and strategies) to help us self-regulate at times of stress. If, however, we haven't had appropriate calming and soothing, at the right time, then our regulatory systems can be over-active and we can end up becoming dysregulated very frequently, even for everyday ordinary stressors. This is why many of our pupils need so much help with regulation.

Relational buffering Rich relational connection serves a protective function. It provides protection from the full impact of stress. It prevents stress from becoming toxic and damaging us. Those who have experienced relational poverty/withdrawal or trauma are very vulnerable and fragile in the midst of everyday ordinary stressors, as well as extraordinary **toxic stress**. This puts them at further risk.

Many of the pupils in our care who have experienced significant **relational trauma** and loss had to manage big overwhelming states, sensations and feelings on their own. Because this occurred when their developing nervous systems were very fragile, they have learned to rely on their feeling brain, and primitive limbic system in relation to stressors that come their way.

The Parent and Carer in School

If we can now stand in the gap and give these pupils the sensitive, attuned care that they didn't have or didn't have enough of in their early years, then we are in effect providing them with the relational buffering they need in order to interrupt the impulsivity that occurs by using the emotional brain in isolation. We can in effect become like 'external brains', lending them our thinking brain to inhibit impulsivity, until they can manage for themselves. Check out the 'handbrain model' on Youtube, by Daniel Siegel.

Relational trauma Trauma experienced by the child on a repeated basis within the context of relationship (often from within early attachments) eg abuse, neglect, violence, intrusion, loss, abandonment and so on. The child may well have experienced overwhelm, powerlessness and terror in the process. The child may well now be completely confused as to the role and purpose of adults, having experienced such overwhelm in their care. It is not surprising therefore that coming into contact with us is going to mean them moving into pseudo-independent states, however caring we may try to be.

Relative dependency This term describes what we may be able to facilitate in schools, in order to give a child who has experienced early relational trauma and loss an opportunity for learning, trust and security through the relationship with a consistent adult who offers sensitive care: in this case, the Key Adult.

Safe space A protected area/space or room full of sensory comfort to support a pupil either to upregulate or downregulate dependent on their state. This space is not used as an area for relational withdrawal or isolation but of time with the Key Adult. There is no expectation there will be talking; the best use of the area is to 'be together'. However both adult and pupil may engage in sensory activites, Theraplay® and PACE. The Key Adult learns the pupil and knows what is needed.

Secondary stress When an individual has experienced profound trauma, those working and living with them are likely to experience stress within their relationships and contact. This stress is a physiological and psychological reality, and those affected will need to seek their own support to help manage it.

Secure attachment This indicates a healthy and appropriate style of relating to other people. An interplay of dependence and independence is observed in response to needs and the satisfaction of those needs, as well as empathy for and generosity towards others.

Secure base A term used by Sir John Bowlby to describe what a 'significant other' (eg. a parent/carer at home, or a Key Adult in school) can become if he or she provides 'good enough' care for a child. It is from this base that a child can become free to explore and engage with the learning process in school. Equally a room with supportive colleagues can provide a 'secure base' for staff (see **attachment system**).

The Parent and Carer in School

Social Engagement System Described by Stephen Porges (*please see* (**STL**) p.80) as the open and engaged state achieved when an individual feels safe, and from which the individual will invite communication, understanding and joint interest in the immediate situation with another person.

Splitting When a child presents with a pattern of disorganised and insecure attachment, the adults around him or her may, in response to the strong feelings stirred up by the child's behaviour and responses, become polarised in their view of him or her and each other. Blame and division can easily develop. Team Pupil and the wider system around the child need to find support so that this 'splitting' can be resolved in the interests of the child and of preserving best working practices and relationships.

Toxic stress We all experience ordinary stressors in life. However if a child with a fragile and developing nervous system experiences extraordinary stressors, for example at the hands of his or her own parents, over a period of time, then the child can move into overwhelm. This overwhelm, which can include being flooded with high levels of stress hormones for significant periods, can put undue pressure on the developing body and brain, heart and mind, meaning that their natural development and functioning may become disrupted. This may lead to the state described as 'developmental vulnerability', or trauma.

References

Aspden, K.L. (2015) *Help! I've got an alarm bell going off in my head! How panic, anxiety and stress affect your body* London: Jessica Kingsley Publishers

Belsky, J., Vandell, D.L., Burchinal, M., Clarke-Stewart, K.A., McCartney, K., Owen, M.P. & The NICHD Early Child Care Research Network (2007) Are There Long-Term Effects of Early Child Care? *Child Development* Vol 78, (2) pp.681-701

Bombèr, L.M. (2007) *Inside I'm Hurting: Practical strategies for supporting children with attachment difficulties in schools* London: Worth Publishing

Bombèr, L.M. (2009) Survival of the fittest: teenagers finding their way through the labyrinth of transitions in schools in, Perry, A. (Ed.) *Teenagers and Attachment: Helping adolescents engage with life and learning* London: Worth Publishing

Bombèr, L.M. (2011) *What About Me? Inclusive strategies to support pupils with attachment difficulties make it through the school day* London: Worth Publishing

Bombèr, L.M. & Hughes, D. (2013) *Settling to Learn: Why relationships matter in schools* London: Worth Publishing

Bombèr, L.M. (2015) *The Key Adult in School, Attachment Aware Schools Series Book 1* Duffield, Derbyshire: Worth Publishing

The Parent and Carer in School

Bombèr, L.M. (2016) *The Senior Manager in School, Attachment Aware Schools Series Book 2* Duffield, Derbyshire: Worth Publishing

Bombèr, L.M. (2016) *The Key Teacher in School, Attachment Aware Schools Series Book 3* Duffield, Derbyshire: Worth Publishing

Booth, P. & Jernberg, A. (2010) *Theraplay: Helping parents and children build better relationships through attachment based play* New York: John Wiley & Sons

Brown, B. (2012) *Daring Greatly: How the courage to be vulnerable transforms the way we live, love, parent and lead* London: Penguin Books Ltd

Brown, B. (2010) *Ted Talk on Vulnerability* ted.com/talks/brene_brown_on_vulnerability?language=en

Cameron, C., Connelly, G. & Jackson, S. (2015) *Educating Children and Young People in Care* London: Jessica Kingsley

Circle of Security youtube clip youtube.com/watch?v=F6DhnbgRAOo Shark Music vimeo.com/145329119

Clarke, J. & Dawson, C. (1998) *Growing Up Again* Minnesota, USA: Hazelden

Cozolino, L. (2013) *The Social Neuroscience of Education: Optimizing attachment and learning in the classroom* New York: WW Norton

Cozolino, L. (2014) *The Neuroscience of Human Relationships: A practical guide for the inner journey* New York: WW Norton

Forbes, H. (2011) *Overwhelm - Beyond Consequences: Parenting Solutions* Youtube v=X9zLKSoYOaO

Forbes, H. (2012) *Help for Billy: A Beyond Consequences approach to helping challenging children in the classroom* Beyond Consequences Institute, LLC. beyondconsequences.com

Geddes, H. (2006) *Attachment in the Classroom*
London: Worth Publishing

Golding, K. (2013) *Nurturing Attachments Training Resource*
London: Jessica Kingsley

Golding, K., Fain, J., Frost, A., Mills, C., Worrall, H., Roberts, N., Durant, E. & Templeton, S. (2012) *Observing Children with Attachment Difficulties in School: A tool for identifying and supporting emotional and social difficulties in children* London: Jessica Kingsley

Golding, K. & Hughes, D. (2012) *Creating Loving Attachments*
London: Jessica Kingsley

Golding, K.S. (2014) *Nurturing Attachments Training Resource. Running Groups for Adoptive Parents and Carers of Children Who Have Experienced Early Trauma and Attachment Difficulties* London: Jessica Kingsley Publishers

Greenhalgh, P. (1994) *Emotional Growth & Learning*
London: Routledge

Gregory, A. & Weinstein, R.S. (2004) Connection and Regulation at Home and in School: Predicting growth in achievement for adolescents *Journal of Adolescent Research* July, Vol 19 (4) pp.405-427

Handford, M. (2104) *Where's Wally?* books UK: Walker Books

Hughes, D. (2004) *Facilitating Developmental Attachment: The road to emotional recovery and behavioural change in foster and adopted children* Maryland, USA: Aronson Inc

Hughes, D. (2009) *Principles of Attachment-Focused Parenting: Effective strategies to care for children*
London: WW Norton

Hughes, D. (2013) *8 Keys to Building your Best Relationships*
New York: WW Norton

Hughes, D. & Baylin, J. (2012) *Brain-Based Parenting: The neuroscience of caregiving for healthy attachment*
New York: WW Norton

The Parent and Carer in School

Hughes, D. (2016) Attachment Conference London: Centre for Child Mental Health, (April)

Johnstone, M. (2012) *Quiet the Mind* London: Robinson

Karst, P. (2000) *The Invisible String* Camarilla, CA: Devorss & Co

Kintsugi youtube.com/watch?v=EBUTQkaSSTY
youtube.com/watch?v=IT55_u8URU0

Magorian, M. (2014) *Goodnight Mr Tom* London: Puffin Classic

Mate, G. (2013) *Attachment and Brain Development* YouTube/v=UbiWLLYSZhc

Music, G. (2011) *Nurturing Natures: Attachment and children's emotional, sociocultural and brain development* Hove: Psychology Press

Music, G. (2014) *The Good Life: Wellbeing and the new science of altruism, selfishness and immorality* Hove, UK: Routledge

Olson, K. (2014) *The Invisible Classroom: Relationships, neuroscience & mindfulness in school* New York: WW Norton

Palmer, S. (2007) *Toxic Childhood* London: Orion

Perry, B. (1999) *Memories of Fear: How the brain stores and retrieves physiologic states, feelings, behaviours and thoughts from traumatic events* Academy version, The Child Trauma Academy Houston, Texas
childtrauma.org/wp-content/uploads/2014/12/Memories_of_Fear_Perry.pdf

Perry, B. (2010) *Born for Love: Why empathy is essential and endangered* New York: Harper Collins Publishers

Perry, B. (2014) *Brain Development and Learning* Columbus Metropolitan Club, Youtube/DXdBFFph2QQ

Powell, B., Cooper, G., Hoffman, K. & Marvin, R. (2013) *The Circle of Security Intervention: Enhancing attachment in early parent-child relationships* New York: Guildford Press

Riley, P. (2011) *Attachment Theory and the Teacher-Student Relationship: A practical guide for teachers, teacher educators and school leaders* Oxon: Routledge

Robinson, K. (2010) *The Element: How finding your passion changes everything* UK: Penguin

Siegel, D. (1999) *The Developing Mind* New York: The Guildford Press

Siegel, D. (2012) The Hand Model of the Brain youtube.com/watch?v=gm9ClJ74Oxw

Siegel, D. & Bryson, T.P. (2012) *The Whole Brain Child: 12 proven strategies to nurture your child's developing mind* London: Robinson

Siegel, D. & Bryson, T.P. (2014) *No-Drama Discipline: The whole brain way to calm the chaos and nurture your child's developing mind* Australia & UK: Scribe

Siegel, D.J. & Bryson, T.P. (2015) *Connect and Redirect Refrigerator Sheet* drdansiegel.com/pdf/Refrigerator%20Sheet--NDD.pdf

Street, K. (2014) *School as a Secure Base: How peaceful teachers can create peaceful schools* London: Worth Publishing

Sunderland, M. (2006) *The Science of Parenting: Practical guidance on sleep, crying, play and building emotional wellbeing for life* London: Dorling Kindersley

Sunderland, M. (2015) *Conversations that Matter: Talking with children and teenagers in ways that help* Derbyshire, UK: Worth Publishing

Sunderland, M. (2016) *Best Relationship with your Child* DVD Series childmentalhealthcentre.org/buy-dvds/category

The Parent and Carer in School

Taransaud, D. (2011) *You Think I'm Evil: Practical strategies for working with aggressive and rebellious adolescents* London: Worth Publishing

Thierry, B. (2015) *Teaching the Child on the Trauma Continuum* Surrey: Grosvenor House Publishing Ltd

Van der Kolk, B. (2014) *The Body Keeps the Score: Brain, mind and body in the healing of trauma* New York, US: Viking

Wetz, J. (2009) *Urban Village Schools: Putting relationships at the heart of secondary school organisation and design UK:* Calouste Gulbenkian Foundation

Wilson, D. & Newton, C. (2006) *Circle of Adults: A team approach to problem solving around challenging behaviour and emotional needs* Nottingham: Inclusive solutions

WiseUp! adoptionsupport.org/store/w-i-s-e-up-powerbook-for-children-in-foster-care

Useful contacts

Attachment Lead Network	attachmentleadnetwork.net
B.A.S.E.® Babywatching UK	base-babywatching-uk.org
Beyond Consequences	beyondconsequences.com
Bruce D. Perry, Psychiatrist	childtrauma.org
Caspari Foundation	caspari.org.uk
Centre for Child Mental Health	childmentalhealthcentre.org
The Centre for Emotional Development	emotionaldevelopment.co.uk
Child Trauma Academy	childtrauma.org
Circle of Security	circleofsecurity.net
Consortium for Emotional Wellbeing in Schools	jameswetz3@gmail.com
Daniel A. Hughes, Child Psychologist	danielhughes.org

The Parent and Carer in School

Dan Siegel, Professor of Psychiatry	drdansiegel.com
Dyadic Development Psychotherapy UK	ddpnetwork.org/uk
Heart Math	heartmath.com
Inclusive Solutions	inclusive-solutions.com
Institute for Arts in Therapy and Education London	artspsychotherapy.org
Institute for Recovery from Childhood Trauma	irct.org.uk
Nurture Group Network	nurturegroups.org
Pets as Therapy	petsastherapy.org
Theraplay®	theraplay.org
Transforming Lives for Good	tlg.org.uk